GEOMETRIX

161 Patterns and Motifs
for Artists and Designers

by

CLARENCE P. HORNUNG

Dover Publications, Inc., New York

Copyright © 1991 by Clarence P. Hornung.
All rights reserved under Pan American and International Copyright Conventions.

Published in Canada by General Publishing Company, Ltd., 30 Lesmill Road, Don Mills, Toronto, Ontario.

Published in the United Kingdom by Constable and Company, Ltd., 3 The Lanchesters, 162–164 Fulham Palace Road, London W6 9ER.

Geometrix: 161 Patterns and Motifs for Artists and Designers is a new work, first published by Dover Publications, Inc., in 1991.

DOVER *Pictorial Archive* SERIES

Manufactured in the United States of America
Dover Publications, Inc., 31 East 2nd Street, Mineola, N.Y. 11501

Library of Congress Cataloging-in-Publication Data

Hornung, Clarence Pearson.
    Geometrix : 161 patterns and motifs for artists and designers / by Clarence P. Hornung.
        p.   cm. – (Dover pictorial archive series)
    ISBN 0-486-26674-5
    1. Borders, Ornamental (Decorative arts)   2. Repetitive patterns (Decorative arts) 3. Stars in art.   4. Polyhedra in art.   I. Title.   II. Series.
NK1570.H595   1991
745.4 – dc20
                                                                                90-28121
                                                                                CIP

INTRODUCTION

IT IS WITH considerable gratification that, after an association of 45 years, I have given Dover Publications the third volume of my trilogy devoted to the study of design, a study that has held my interest since 1920, when I entered the field of graphic design. The first of these books, the *Handbook of Designs and Devices* (20125-2), originally published in 1932, was reprinted by Dover in 1946; *Allover Patterns for Designers and Craftsmen* (23179-8) followed in 1975.

In this volume, I present a blueprint for geometrical patterns made according to fundamental principles.

Before we can create design compositions, it is necessary to establish the essential "alphabet" of visual expression. The vocabulary of the designer is vast in scope and complex in its ramifications. While the writer has only "twenty-six soldiers of lead to conquer the world," the designer has the freedom to create his own motifs from a world of geometric forms and shapes capable of endless variations and applications.

Three devices have been used to create the patterns reproduced in this book:

1. THE MODULE. I have composed my basic units — my modules — of linear strips or striated bands, often modified by angular inserts to add interest. These are contained within triangles, rectangles and rhombuses — forms that offer the greatest potential for mosaic patterning and other design compositions.

2. THE GRID. Diagrammatic layouts following triangular, rectangular and rhombic forms provide the structural framework into which modular units can be positioned for design compositions.

3. THE PATTERN. When modular units are positioned according to the grid plan, the resultant allover pattern may be extended in all directions.

The designs shown on the following pages are not intended as a substitute for the designer's ingenuity and creativity. Out of his own fertile imagination he must devise his own vocabulary that will express his originality.

C.P.H.
January 1991

CONTENTS

THE BAND

THE BAND OR BORDER is a useful decorative form, not only in architecture but in mural painting, mosaic floor patterns, inlays, marquetry, parquetry, textile bands, weaving, quiltmaking and many varied crafts. By extension, a band, stripe, rim or margin marks the outer edge of an enclosure or a separation between horizontal belt courses. In the applied arts and crafts a band serves to mark a break in areas of construction or composition. All borders may be used horizontally or vertically and applied interchangeably.

The use of a band to enclose the four sides of a rectangular area involves the question of corner treatment. Borders composed of a few simple elements may be mitered, but where modular units are more complex this is not advisable. It is suggested that extraneous though harmonious units be inserted at the corners, and bands abut the corners abruptly. Here, again, the designer's ingenuity comes into play to find the ideal solution, generally the result of experimentation and exploration.

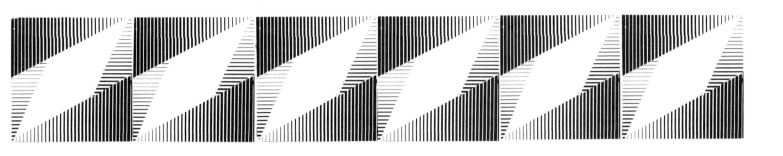

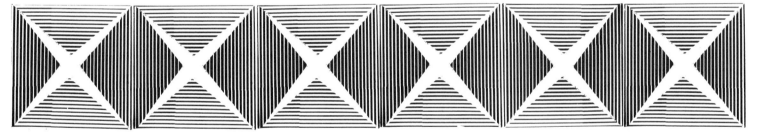

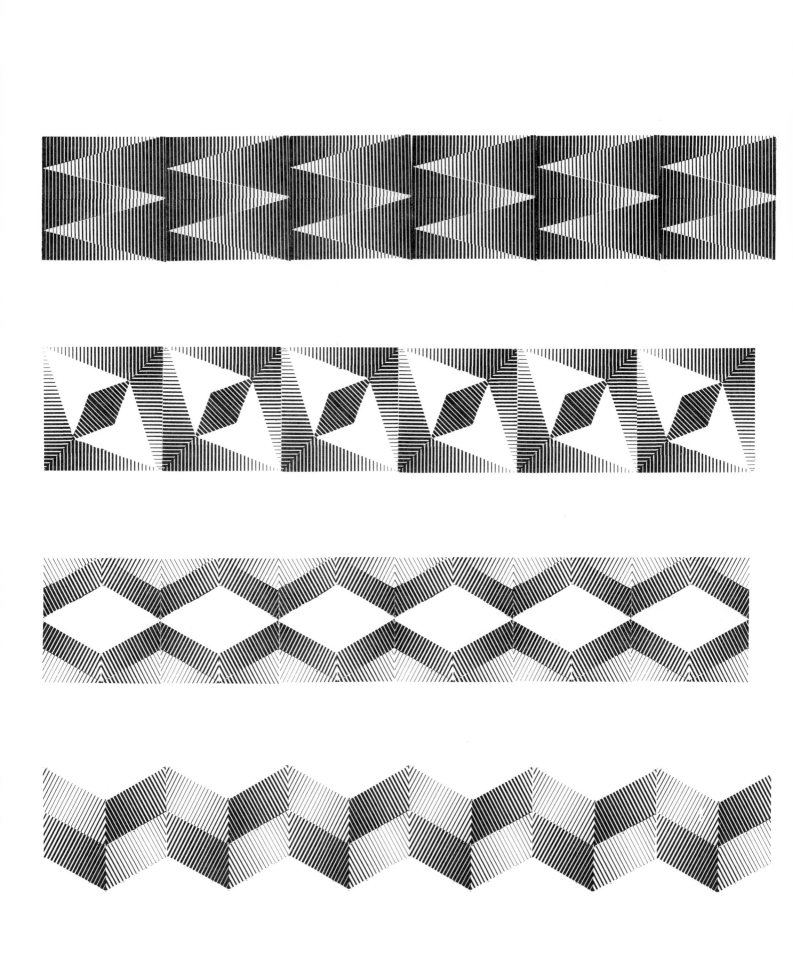

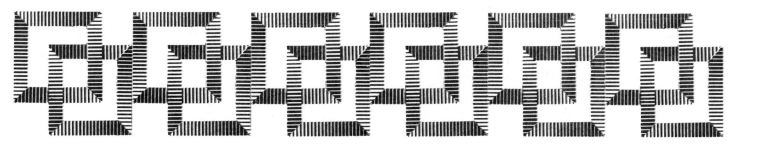

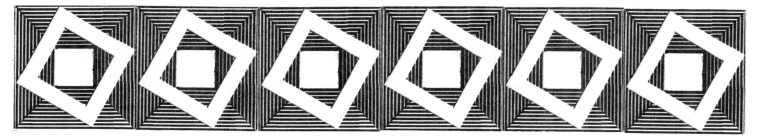

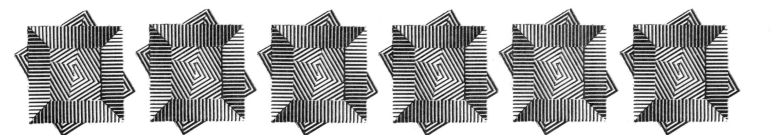

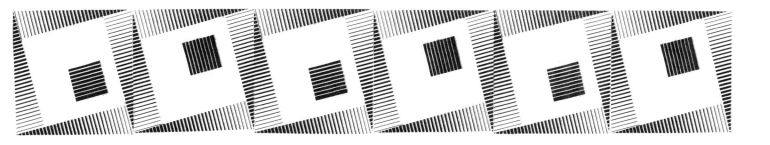

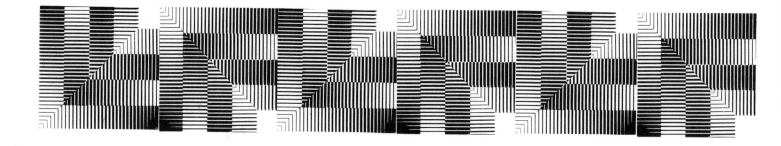

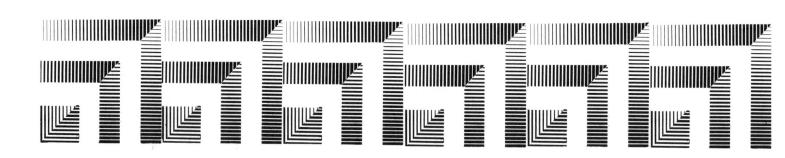

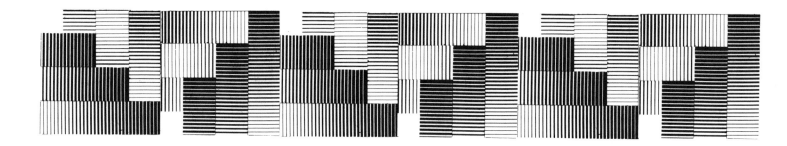

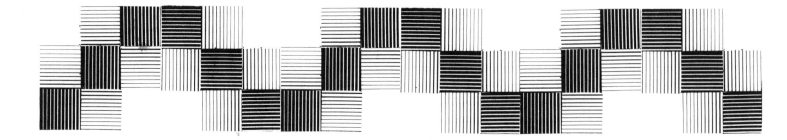

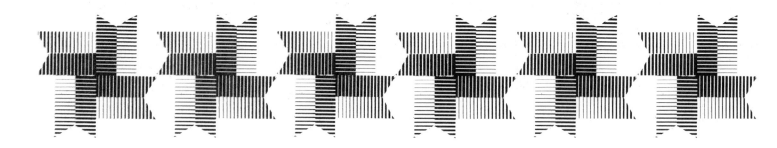

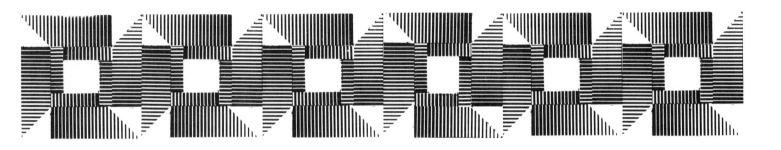

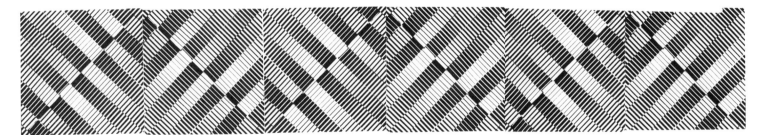

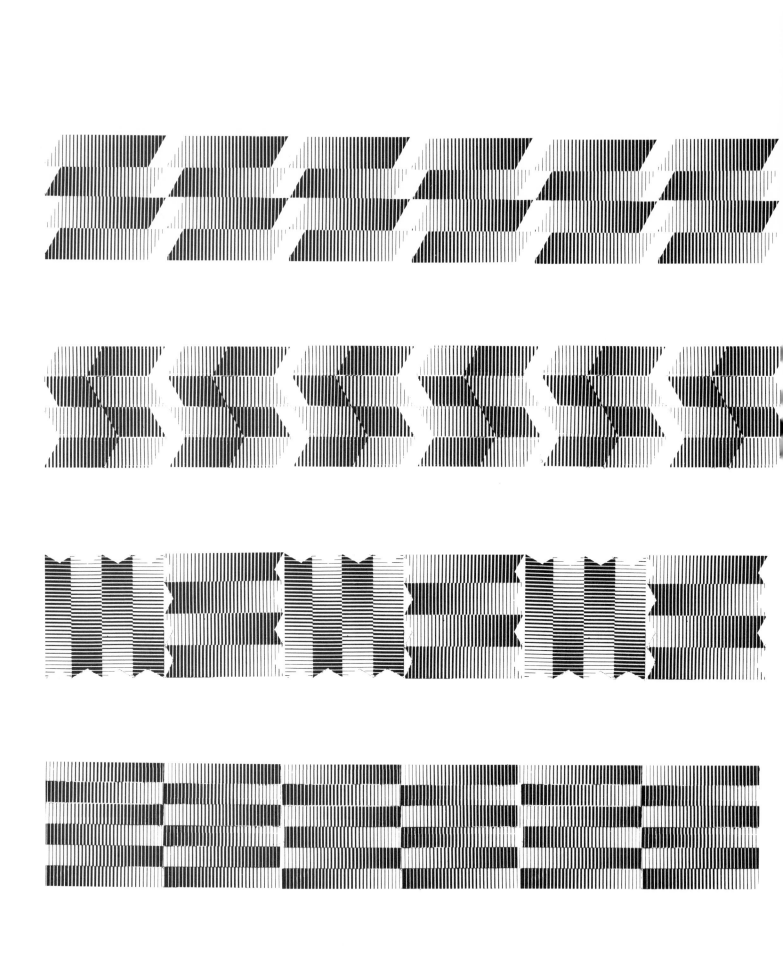

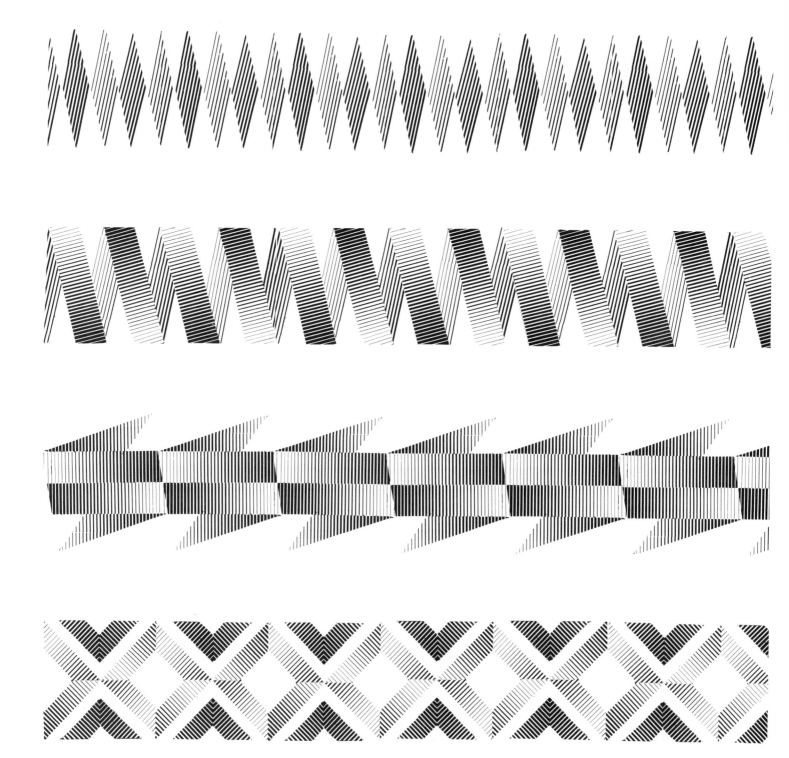

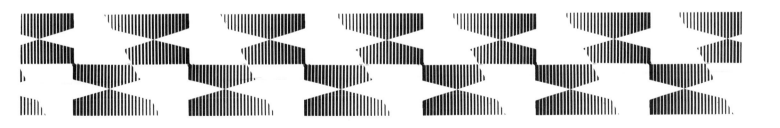

THE PATTERN

PATTERN EXPRESSES man's innate need for ornamentation. We have been able to trace the development of design across all geographic areas and within ethnic groups. We can follow the evolution of design from early cultures to more sophisticated societies.

Patterning may be found in early woven materials such as plaids, diapered cottons and woolens handwoven on crude looms and racks. In Greek and Roman architecture we find ample use of elaborate geometrically patterned floor mosaics. Centuries later, the spread of Islam opened another important chapter in the extensive application of geometrical design. Patterns became more intense and complex, the coloring more brilliant and the scale more magnificent.

The Renaissance was marked by widespread patterning in ceramics and tiling, as well as in woodcraft in its many forms — parquetry, marquetry and intarsia — all of which provide rich examples of geometry's universality.

Finally, various printing techniques produce patterns for wallpapers, wrapping papers, binding papers and an endless number of special designs for special tasks. The uses of allover patterns are being expanded constantly as modern technology creates new needs.

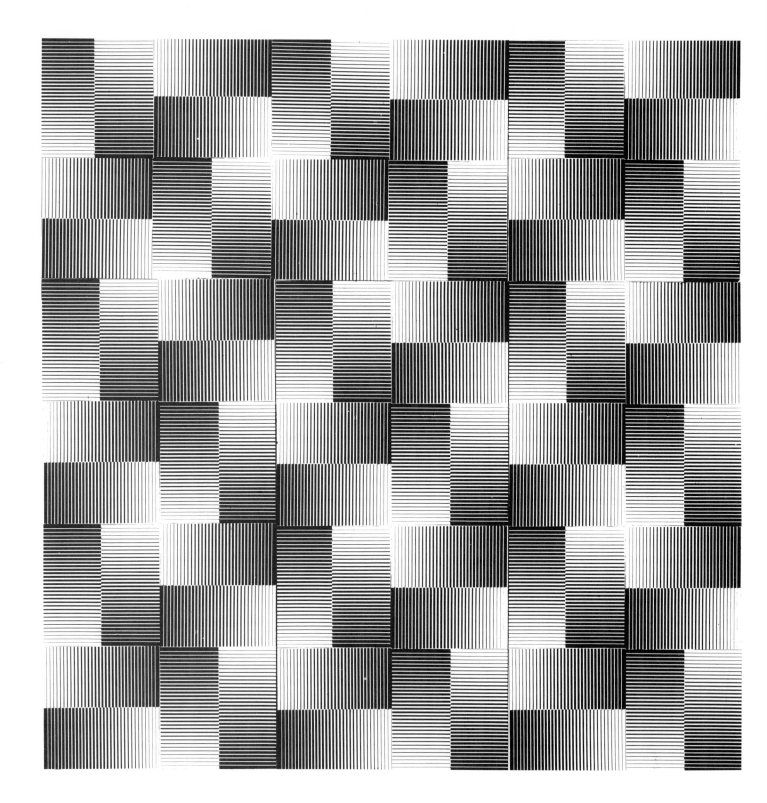

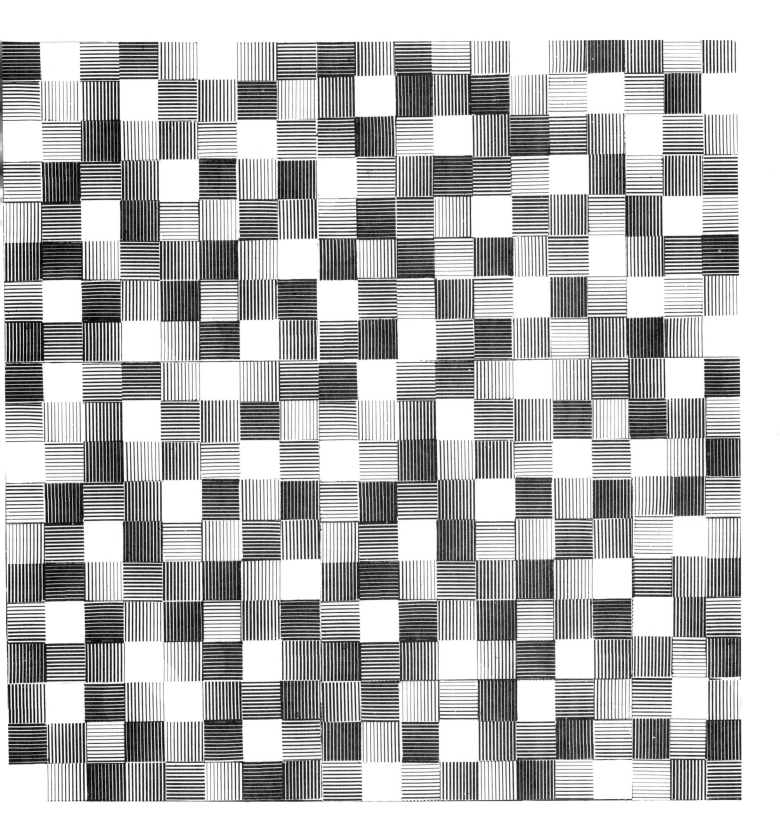

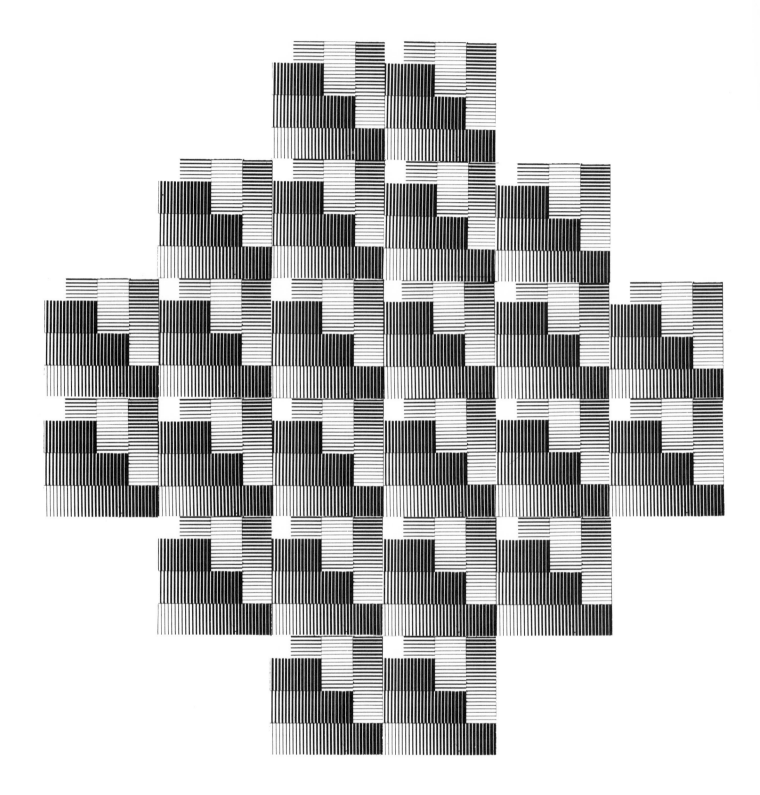

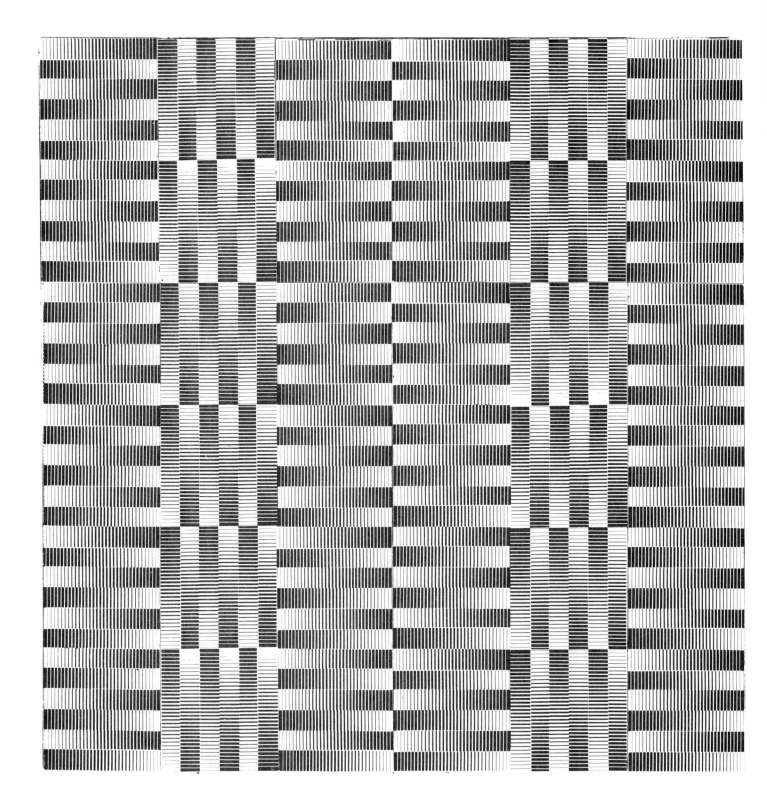

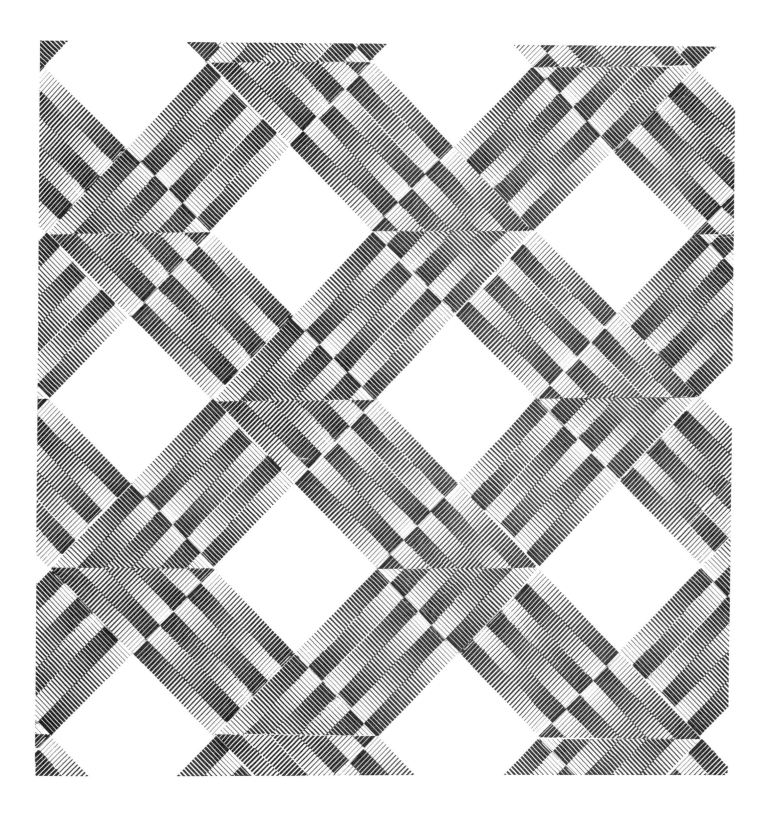

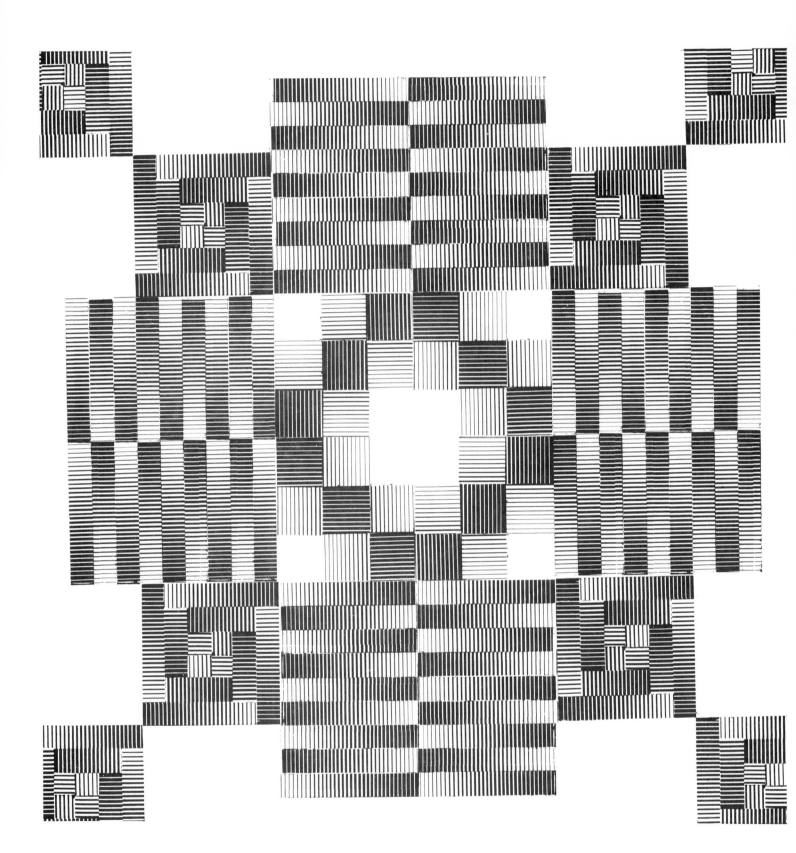

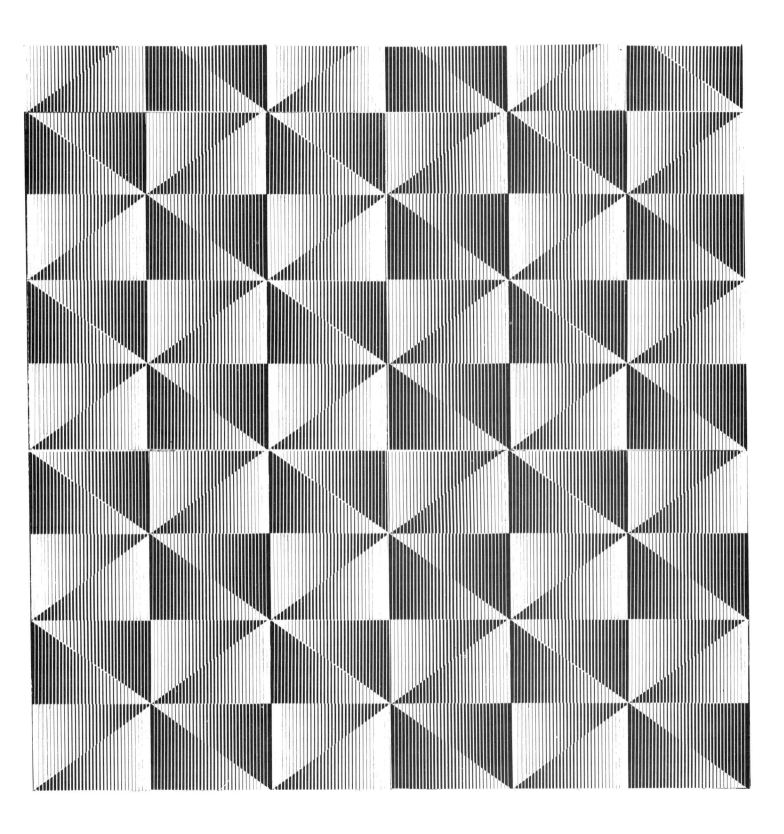

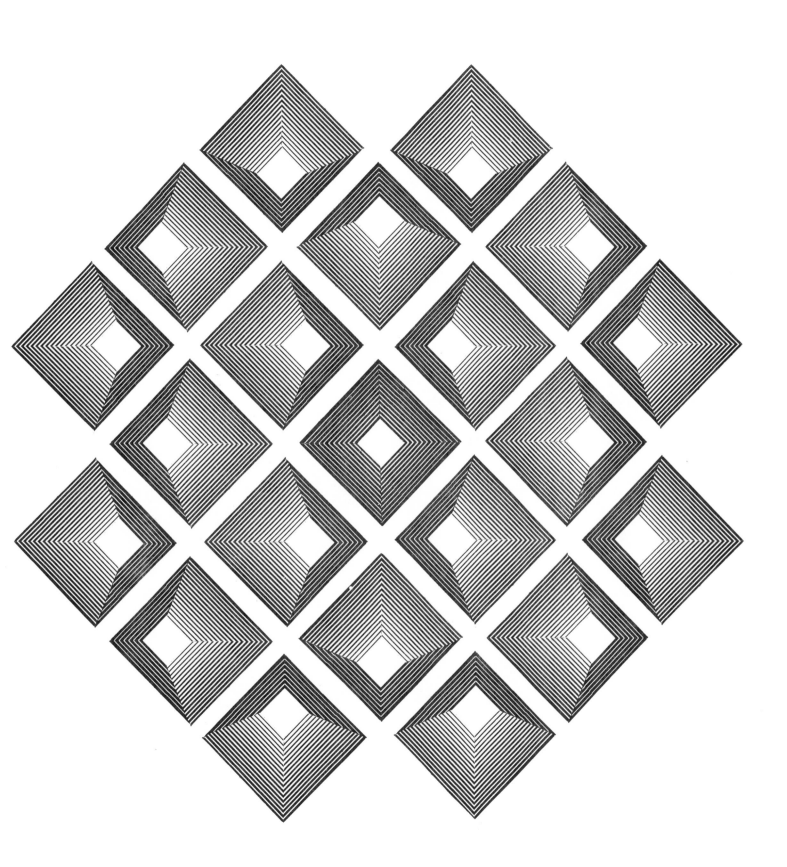

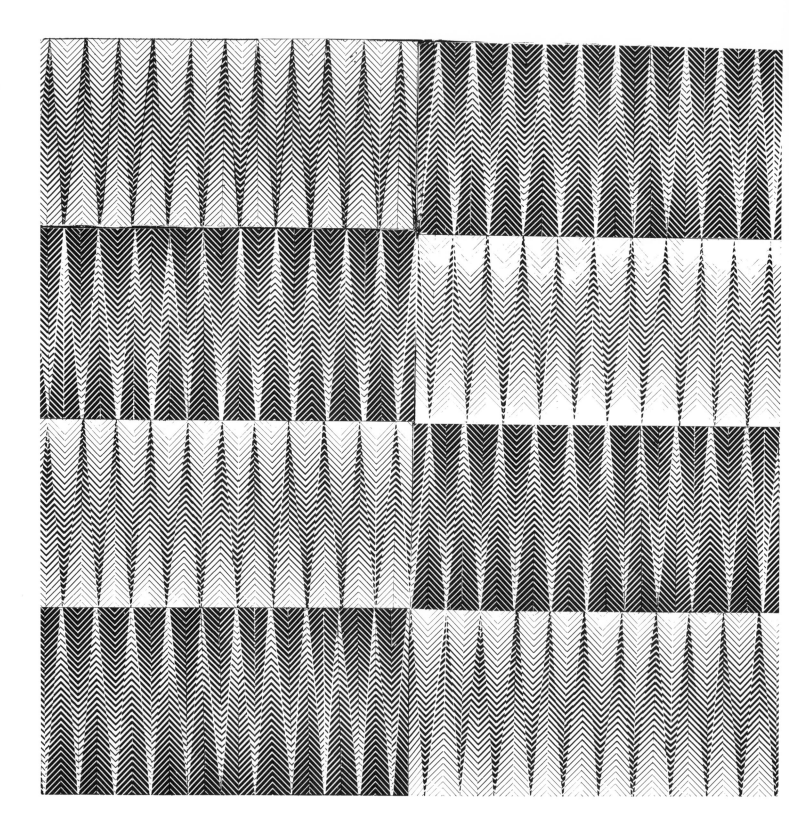

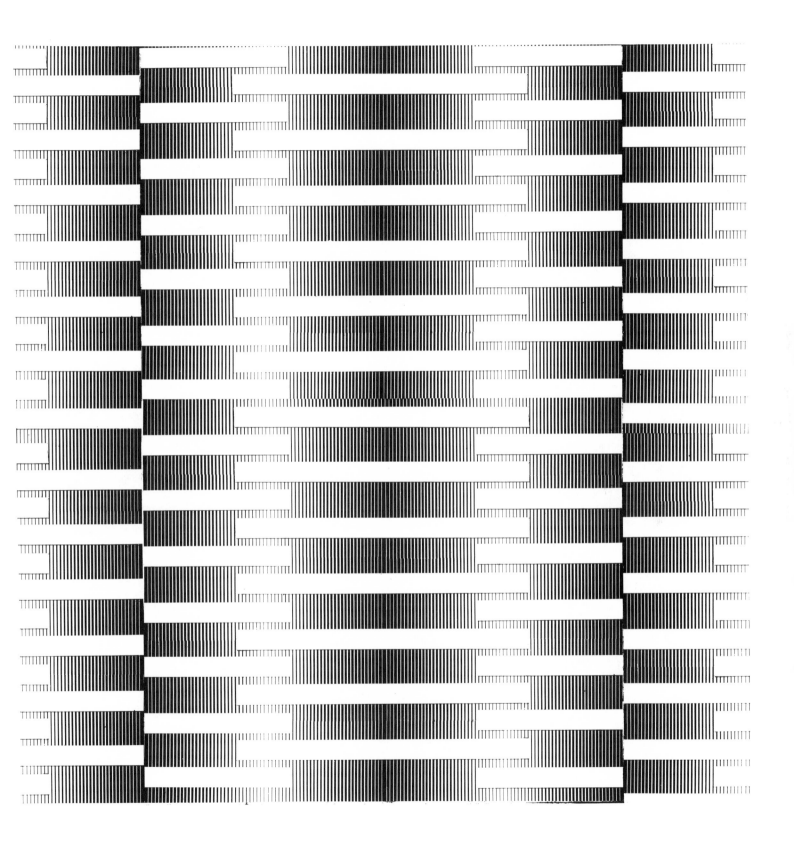

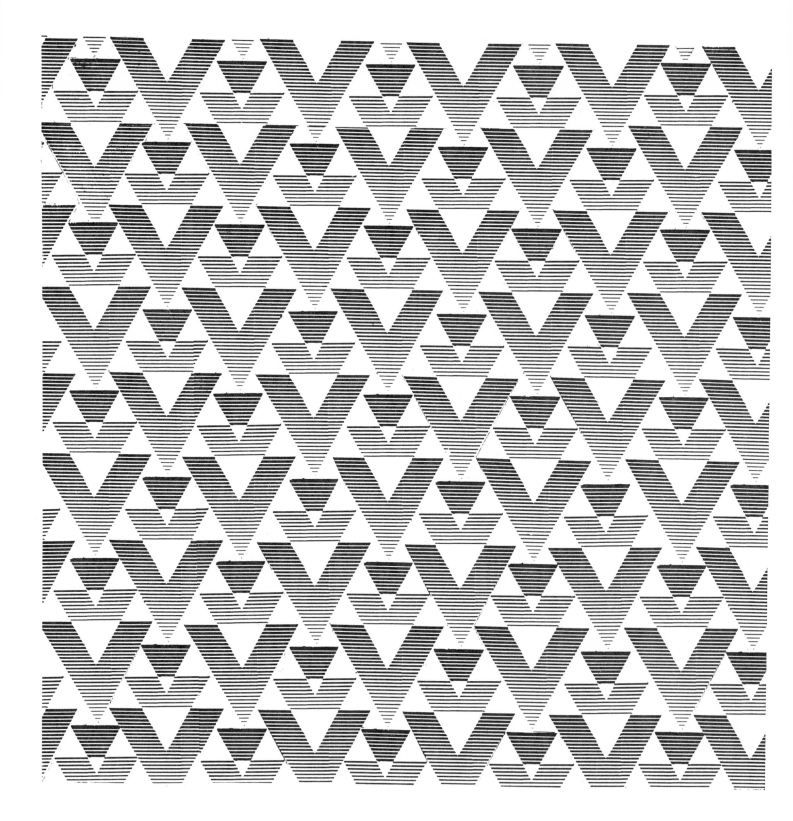

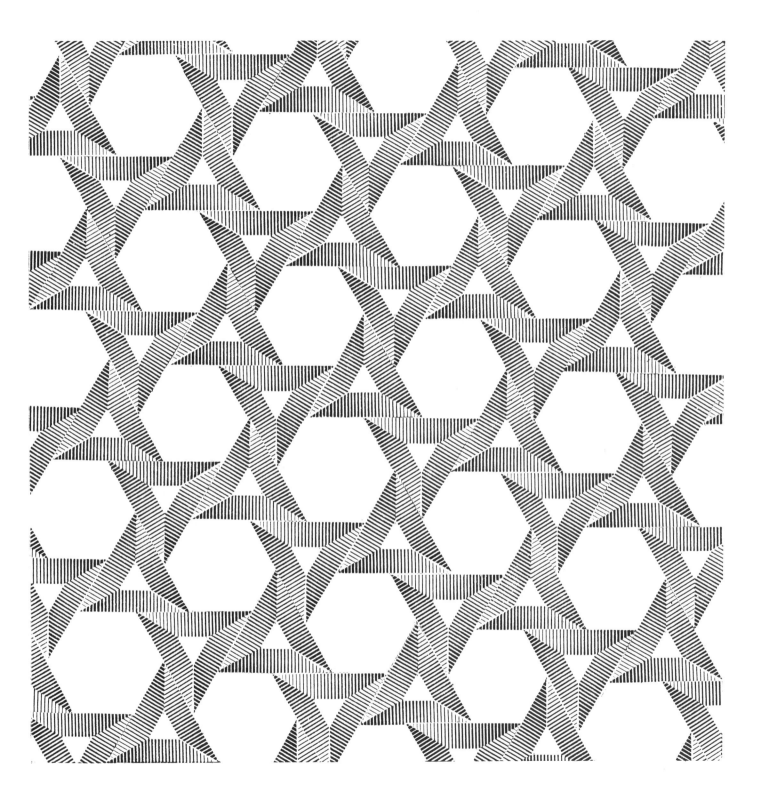

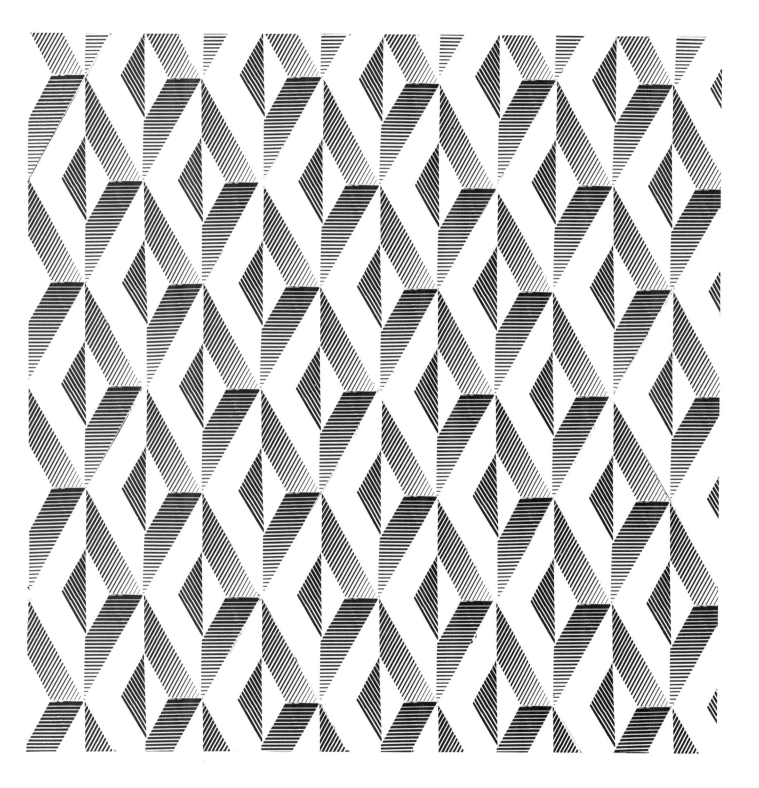

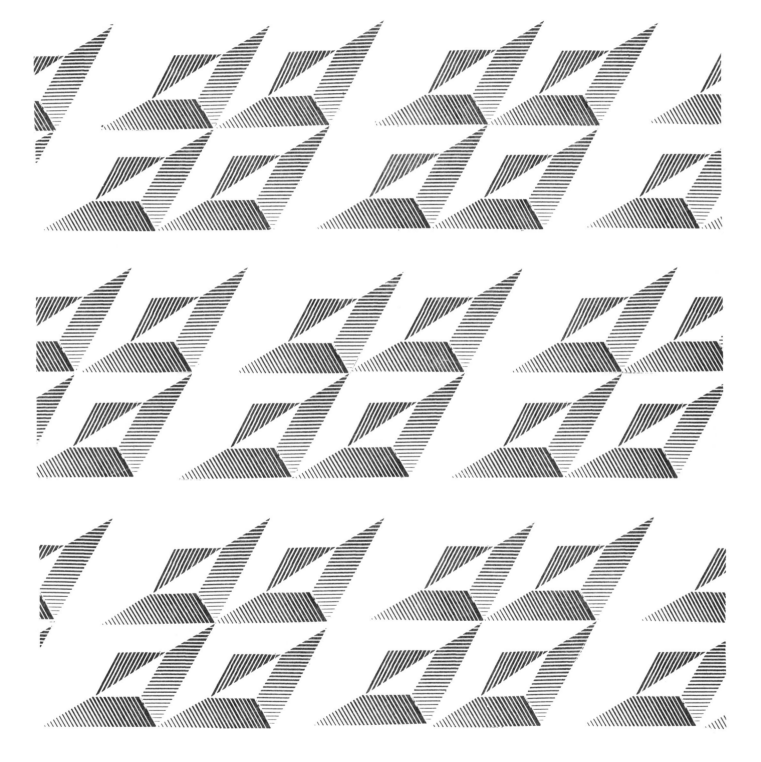

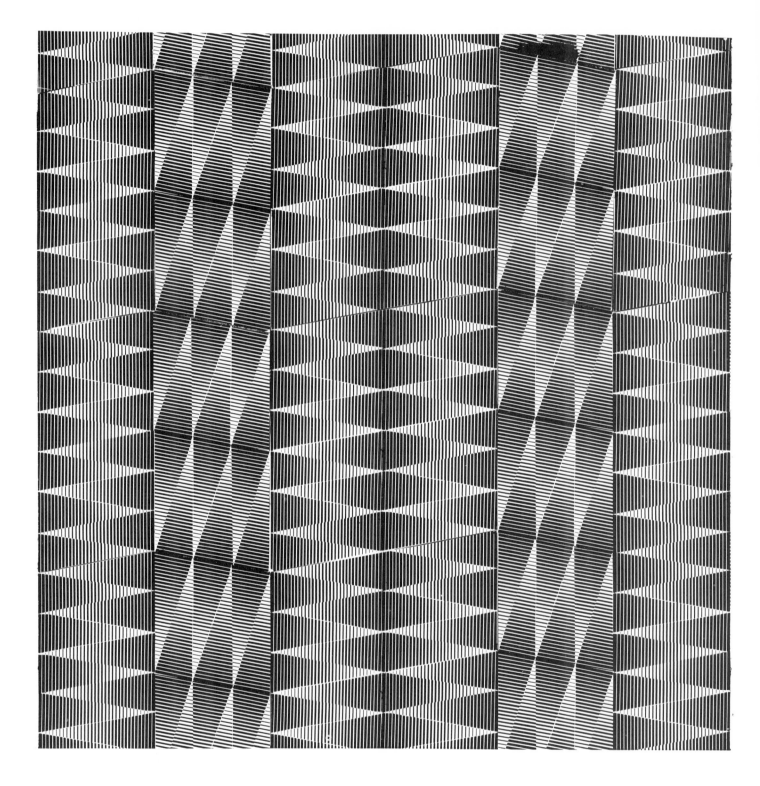

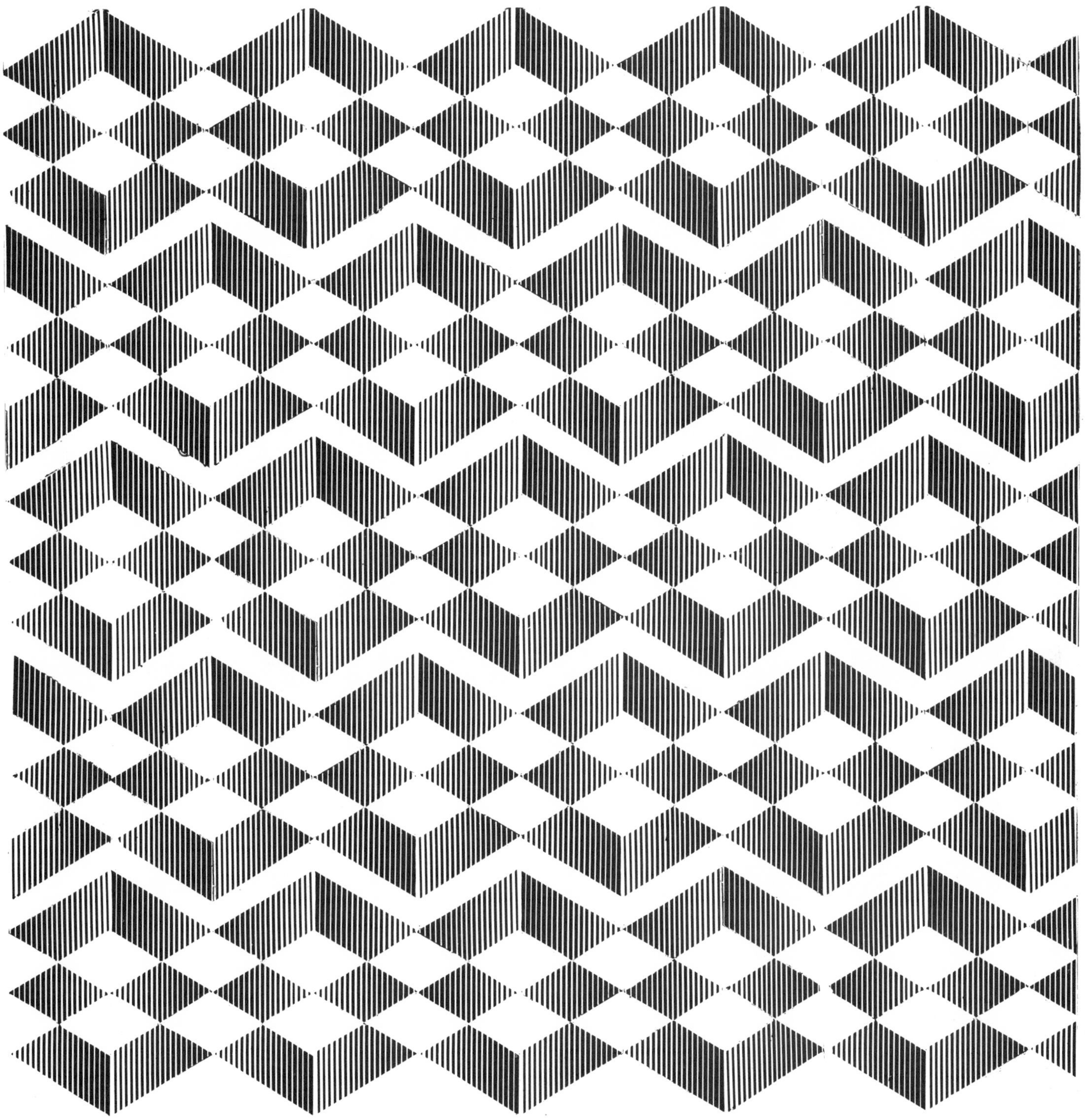

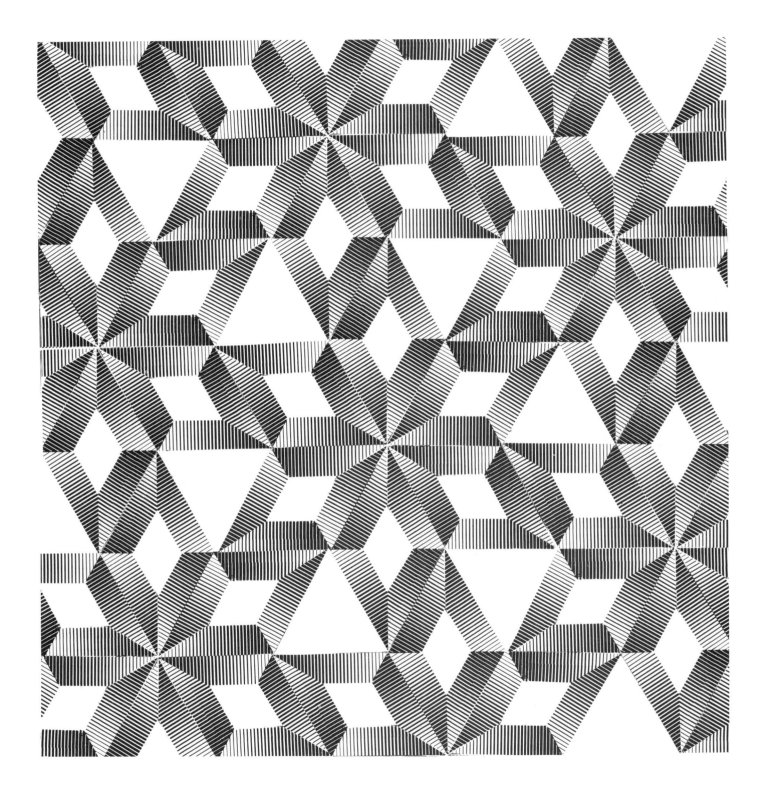

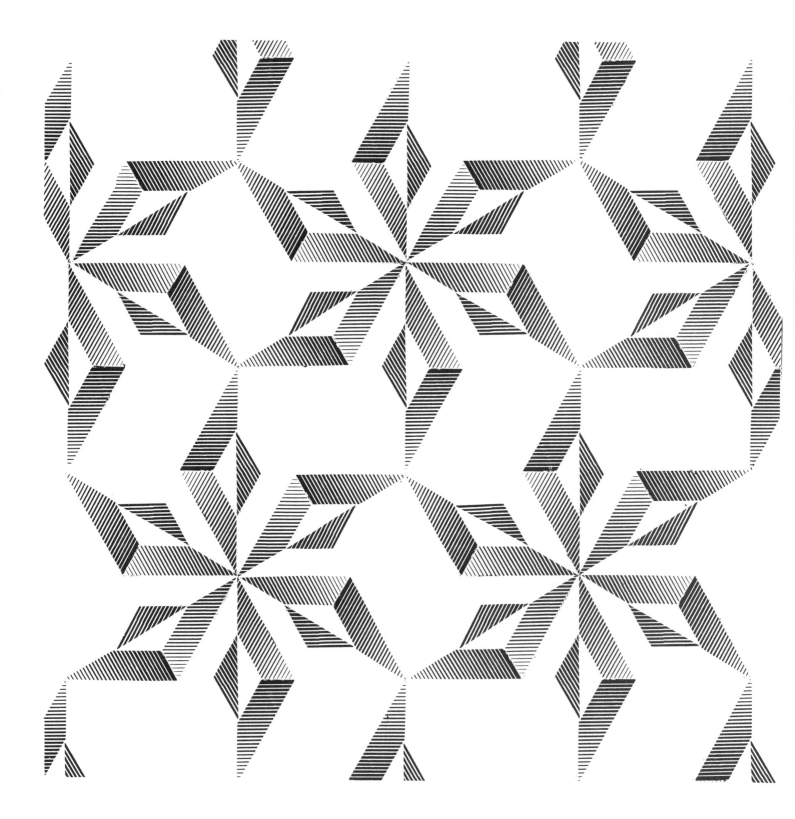

THE STAR

THE STAR form in its many variations has always been a decorative device of prime importance. Structurally, the star assumes many characteristics in great variety, but its essential composition revolves about a central focus of any number of radial arms, like spokes of a wheel emanating from a hub. It may be constructed of as few as three radial axes but most commonly of five or six. Four arms and multiples of 8, 12 and 16 constitute complex forms often referred to by the name rose compass because of resemblance to the face of a compass with its directional divisions.

In ancient Greek temples the naos often featured a star design in its center. Circular Roman temples carried on the floor level a mosaic centerpiece of stellar design. Pompeiian residential atria displayed outstanding mosaic star forms, strictly geometrical in composition.

Many imposing castles and châteaux built throughout Europe starting in the late Renaissance utilize the star in a totally different area: displayed in the fine hardwood floors, especially in public assembly rooms and grand ballrooms. These elaborate examples of parquetry are unique in their complexity and ingenuity.

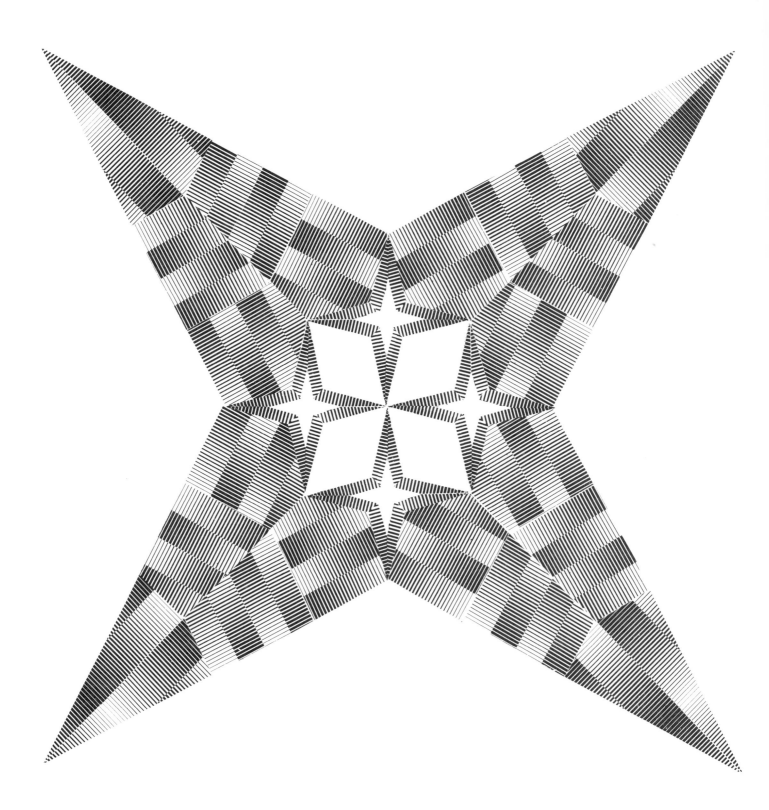

86   The Star

88   The Star

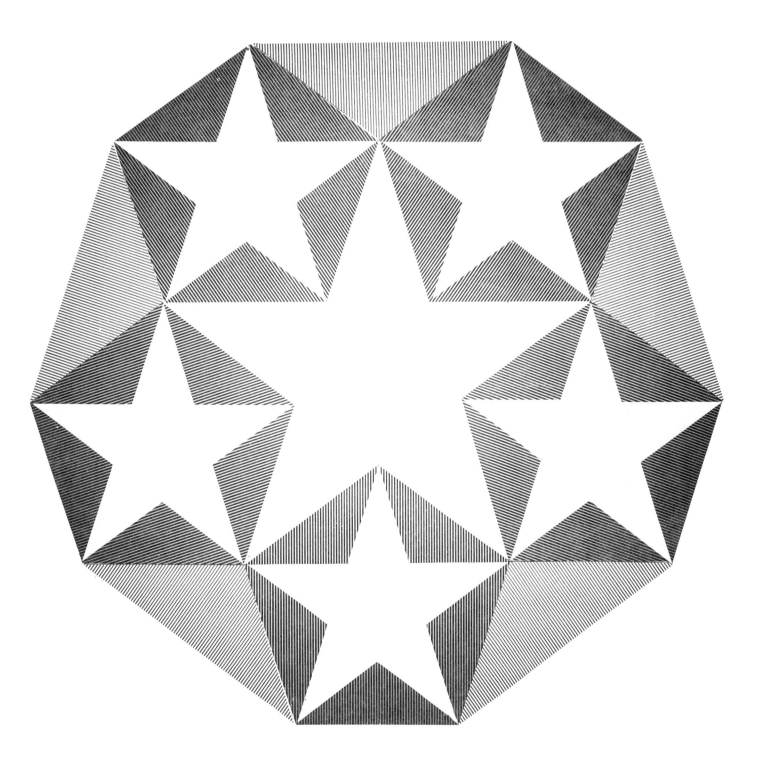

94   The Star

THE SOLID

WE NOW TURN our attention from flat two-dimensional figures to "solid" geometrical forms, called polyhedra, which present new opportunities for experimentation in design.

Nature's examples exist in the domain of minerals and crystals. Geometrical solids were first explored by the ancient Greeks, led by Pythagoras. Almost two centuries later (ca. 350 B.C.), Plato and his school studied what have become known as the Platonic solids: the tetrahedron, with four faces of equal equilateral triangles; the cube, whose six plane surfaces are of equal squares; the octahedron, bounded by eight faces of equal equilateral triangles and shaped like a top with apexes at both ends; the dodecahedron, whose 12 planes are equal regular pentagons; the icosahedron, another top-shaped solid, whose 20 plane surfaces are equal equilateral triangles.

On the following pages, one can observe the inherent beauty of polyhedra. While the Greek geometricians have provided us with the basic forms, their primary concern was with philosophy; interest in these forms as objects of beauty was developed by Islamic civilizations.

100   The Solid

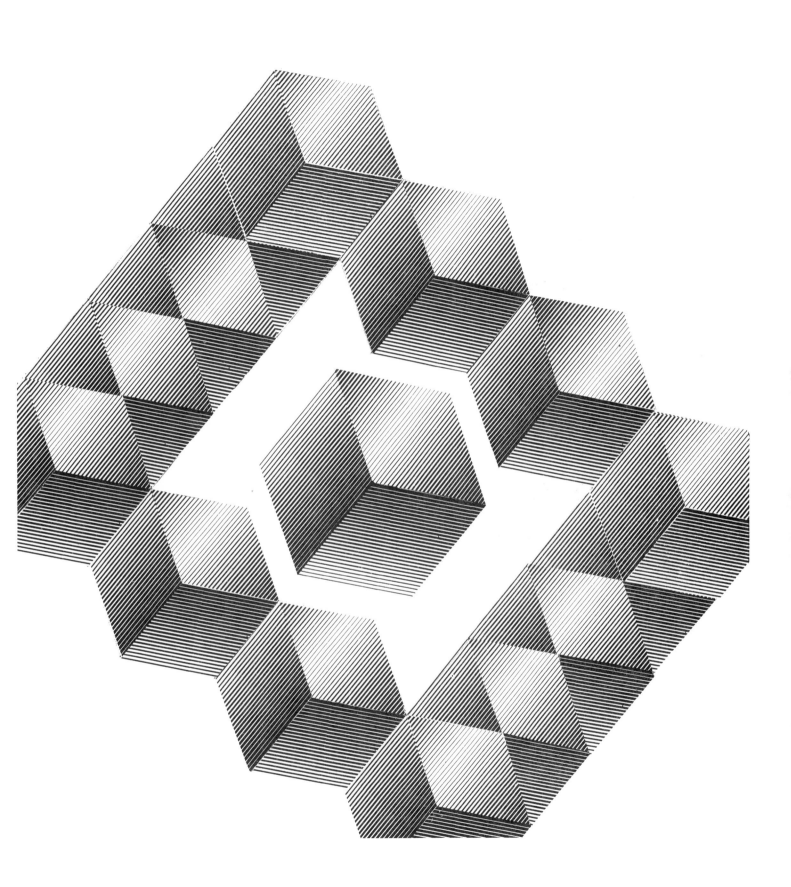

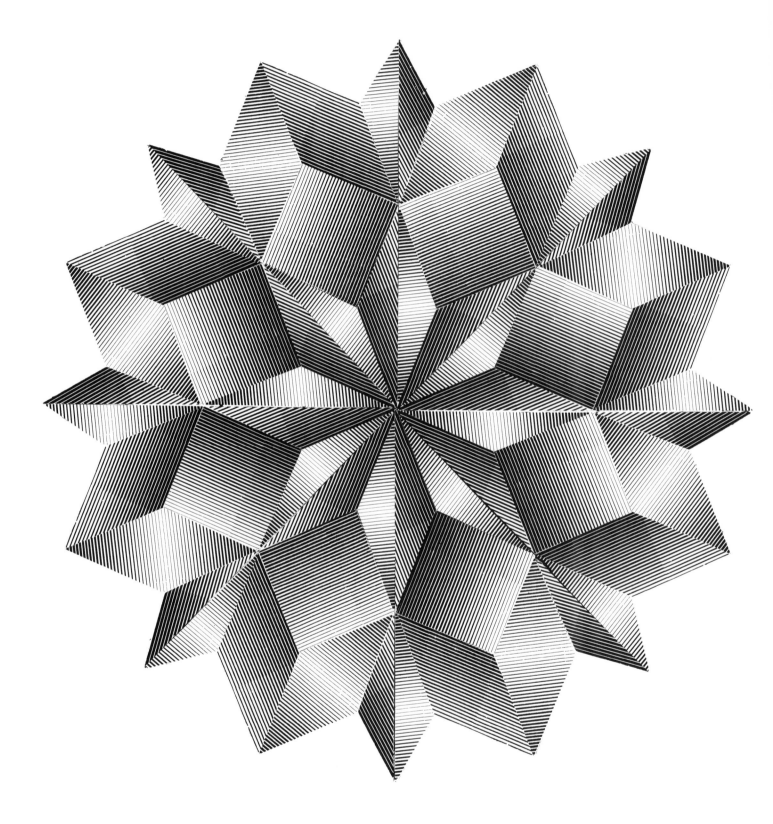

106   The Solid

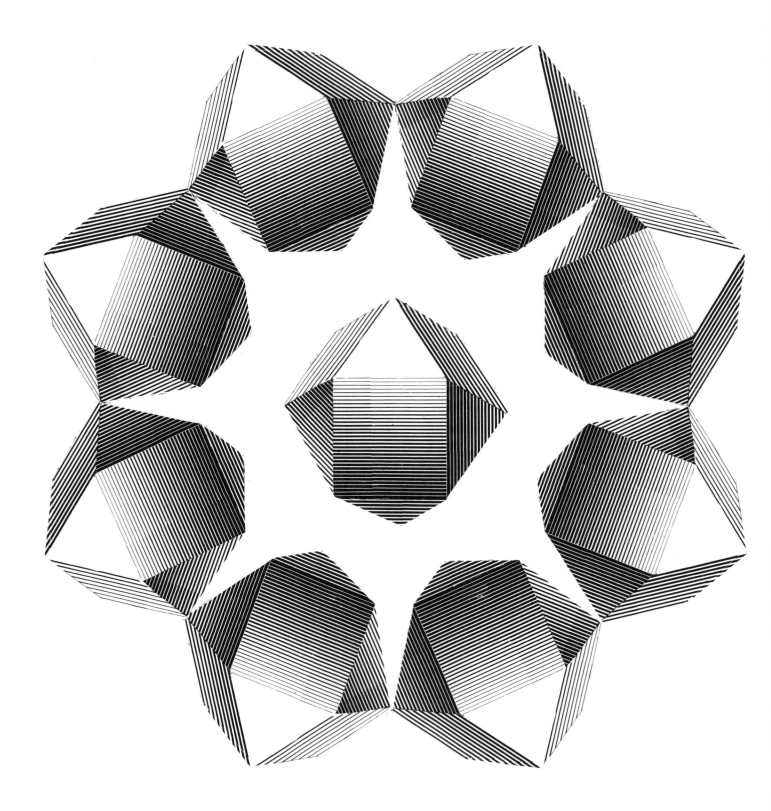

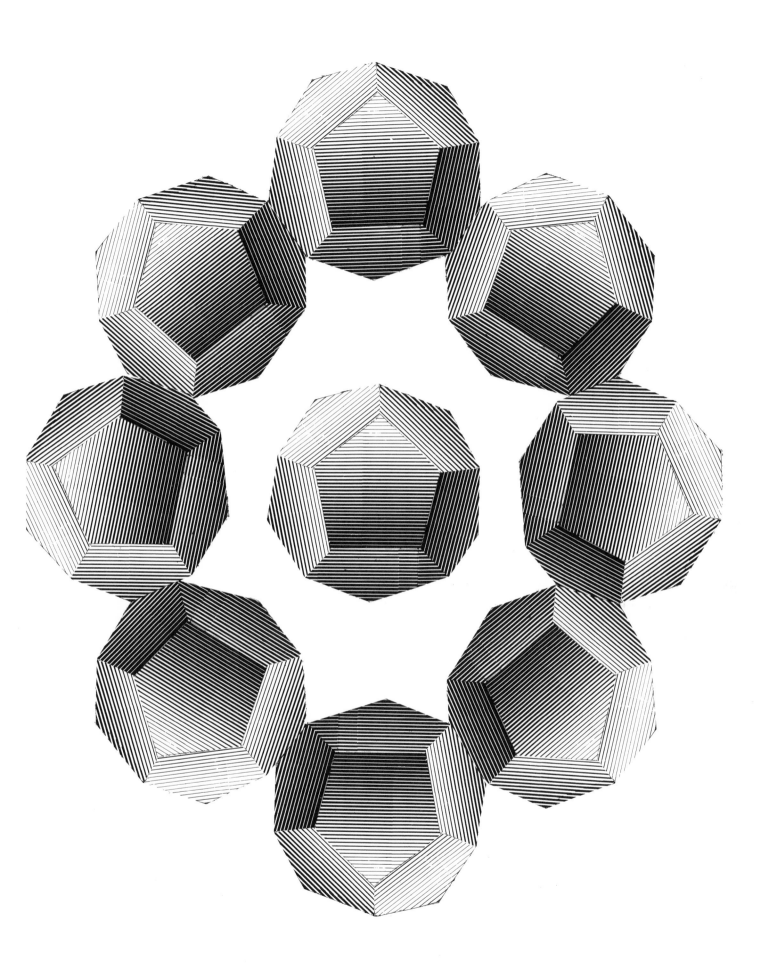